My Muslim Friend

A Young Catholic Learns About Islam

Written by Donna Jean Kemmetmueller, FSP

Illustrated by Laura Jacobsen

With a Foreword by Reverend Canon Francis V. Tiso

Pauline
BOOKS & MEDIA
Boston

Nihil Obstat:
Rev. Raymond G. Helmick, S.J.

Imprimatur:
✠ Most Rev. Seán O'Malley, O.F.M. Cap.
Archbishop of Boston
October 11, 2005

Library of Congress Cataloging-in-Publication Data

Kemmetmueller, Donna Jean.
  My Muslim friend : a young Catholic learns about Islam / written by Donna Jean Kemmetmueller ; illustrated by Laura Jacobsen ; with a foreword by Francis V. Tiso.
      p. cm.
  ISBN 0-8198-4844-1 (hardcover)
  1. Islam--Juvenile literature. 2. Muslims--Juvenile literature. I. Jacobsen, Laura. II. Tiso, Francis. III. Title.
  BP161.3.K357 2006
  297.2'83--dc22
                          2005038033

Texts of the New Testament used in this work are taken from *The New Testament: St. Paul Catholic Edition,* translated by Mark A. Wauck, copyright © 2000 by the Society of St. Paul, Staten Island, New York, and are used by permission. All rights reserved.

Texts of the Qur'an used in this work are taken from *The Qur'an Translation,* translated by Abdullah Yusuf Ali, eleventh edition, 2003, published by Tahrike Tarsile Qur'an, Inc., Publishers and Distributors of Holy Qur'an, 80–08 51st Avenue, Elmhurst, NY 11373, and are used by permission.

Photographs: pp. 20-21, Mary Emmanuel Alves, FSP; pp. 24, 26, 35, 36, 38, Armanda Lawrence Santos, FSP

Published by Pauline Books & Media, 50 Saint Paul's Avenue, Boston, MA 02130-3491.

Printed in Korea.

www.pauline.org

Pauline Books & Media is the publishing house of the Daughters of St. Paul, an international congregation of women religious serving the Church with the communications media.

1 2 3 4 5 6 7 8 9   11 10 09 08 07 06

To *Randa Kuziez,*
my Muslim friend

Foreword

There is an old proverb that states, "Those who fail to study the past will be condemned to repeat it." Less known, but equally neglected, would be the reverse side of that proverb: "Those who fail to plan for the future will have none."

Many dedicated educators, clergy, and community leaders have begun to plan an American future for all who have come here recently, building upon the labors and struggles of those who have been here for a long time. Initiatives in interreligious dialogue have been a significant part of that planning. In the three regional Muslim-Catholic dialogues co-sponsored by the United States Conference of Catholic Bishops, the ways in which our respective communities will live together in peace have begun to bear fruit. The dialogue groups have produced consensus documents on spirituality ("Friends and Not Adversaries: A Catholic-Muslim Spiritual Journey" on the website www.usccb.org), on divine revelation (*Revelation: Catholic and Muslim Perspectives*, USCCB, 2006), and, we hope soon, on marriage and family life. We know that documents are only a start. Documents must inspire reflection, and reflection must produce concrete, reciprocal action.

One of the arenas of action that is perennially dear to both the Catholic and the Muslim communities is the education of the young, and particularly, their spiritual formation. The network of Catholic schools has made and continues to make an extraordinary historic contribution to American life. Similarly, the Muslim communities now active and visible in American cities are constructing schools based on Islamic values and principles. Both systems seek to instruct our young people in accordance with the highest academic standards. Both systems emphasize faith as a sound basis for a truly human life, in which achievement is crowned doubly with ethics and with sacred meaning. Young men and women graduate from these schools with unique abilities to express themselves in depth and conviction, and have shown themselves capable of outstanding leadership in all fields.

Education has to start somewhere. In this beautiful story of friendship between two middle school girls, Sister Donna Jean Kemmetmueller gives us much more than catechesis. This simple tale is a true example of narrative theology, in which friendship leads to greater understanding of the ways by which faith illuminates a human life. Yes, the lights go on, and we find ourselves transformed.

With our Holy Father, Pope Benedict XVI, we discover how Christians and Muslims can be "dear and esteemed friends" able to "face together the many challenges of our time," including the challenge of peacemaking. "The lessons of the past must help us to avoid repeating the same mistakes. We must seek paths of reconciliation and learn to live with respect for each other's identity" ("Meeting with Representatives of Some Muslim Communities," August 20, 2005). May this small book be for our children a first step on a hopeful journey.

Reverend Canon Francis V. Tiso, Ph.D.
Associate Director
Secretariat for Ecumenical and Interreligious Affairs
United States Conference of Catholic Bishops

A Christian is a follower of Jesus Christ. Christians believe that Jesus is the Son of God who became man. He lived in Galilee and Judea around 2,000 years ago. In the Christian religion, Jesus is both true God and true man. By his life, teaching, death, and resurrection, he taught people to love as God loves. Jesus inaugurated the kingdom of God on earth. Christians believe that because Jesus is God, he healed people and forgave their sins.

Hi! My name is Mary. I'm a Catholic Christian.

*I*n Christianity, Mary is the virgin Mother of Jesus and, therefore, the Mother of God. She is a prominent figure in the Christian religion, especially for Catholics. Many Christian girls are named after her.

A Muslim is a follower of the religion called Islam. "Islam" is derived from the Arabic root *s-l-m,* which means "to submit or surrender." The word for peace, *salaam,* is derived from the same root. Islam is a religion that seeks to cultivate peace in one's life through submission, or surrender, to God. Muslims strive to give themselves wholeheartedly to God in a commitment that holds nothing back, and that resists greed, anxiety, and the desire for personal status.

At school, I met Aisha. She's a Muslim.

One of the first things I noticed when I met Aisha was her *hijab,* or headscarf. When I got to know her better, I asked her about it. She told me that last year, soon after she turned twelve, she decided to begin wearing the *hijab.* For a Muslim woman, wearing the *hijab* is an outward sign of faith. It's a commitment that's important to Aisha.

Aisha, a name that means "she who lives" in Arabic, was a wife of Muhammad, the prophet of Islam who lived nearly 1,400 years ago. Many Muslim girls are named after Aisha.

Jews and Christians trace God's covenant with them through Isaac, while Muslims trace their heritage back through Ishmael. The Prophet Muhammad was a descendant of Abraham and Ishmael. Jesus was descended from King David, who was a descendant of Abraham and Isaac.

Three of the world's greatest religions—Judaism, Christianity, and Islam—claim Abraham, known for his supreme trust in the one God, as a father in faith. In Islam he is especially revered as the champion of monotheism, the belief in one God.

God appeared to Abraham and made a covenant (an agreement) with him, promising him blessings and numerous descendants. Abraham gave testimony to his faith in God by leaving his country at God's command.

When Sarah, Abraham's wife, could not bear him a son, she asked him to have a child with Hagar, her maidservant. This was a common practice in Abraham's time. Hagar gave birth to Ishmael. Then Sarah conceived, and Abraham's second son, Isaac, was born. According to the Bible, Sarah demanded, after a rivalry, that Hagar and Ishmael be banished, so Abraham sent them away. God, however, promised Abraham that he would bless Ishmael and his descendants.

Aisha and I see each other almost every day. We're in the same homeroom in seventh grade, and we play on the same soccer team. We've been spending a lot of time together after school, too.

One of the main things Muslims, Christians, and Jews have in common is their belief in the God of Abraham. At a time when people believed in many gods, the one true God revealed himself to Abraham, giving birth to religions that are monotheistic, professing belief in one God.

Did you know?

Although Muslims, Christians, and Jews all worship the one true God, their doctrines about God vary.

We have a lot in common. But we're also very different.

Here are some ways
that Aisha and I are alike:
We're both girls, we were both born in the United States,
we each have one brother, and we both love to ride
horses. Most importantly, we both believe in one God.

The way that each of the three great faith traditions understands God differs. Muslims call God "Allah," which is an Arabic word formed by joining the words "al" (meaning "the") and "Ilah" (meaning "God"). Allah is not *a* god among others, but, literally, "*the* God." Jews also believe in one God.

Christians believe that the one God is a Trinity: three Persons, one in being. The Father, Son, and Holy Spirit—three unique, coequal, and coeternal Persons—are one God.

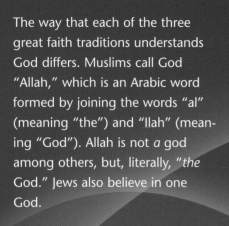

Here are some ways that Aisha and I are different: We live on different streets. We ride different buses to school. She has brown eyes, and mine are blue. Aisha likes vegetables, but I mostly don't!

When Aisha prays, she calls God "Allah." I pray in the name of the Father, and of the Son, and of the Holy Spirit. As a Christian, I believe there is one God in three divine Persons. We call this great mystery the Holy Trinity.

Jesus, the compassionate Son of God, began his public ministry when he was about thirty years old. For approximately three years, he preached, taught, and healed, showing special concern for those seen as social outcasts. Jesus' teachings stirred up controversies that ultimately led to his arrest and execution by crucifixion.

Christians call the union of Jesus' divine and human natures the Incarnation. The Incarnation came about through the power of the Holy Spirit. The Angel Gabriel came to the Virgin Mary and announced that she would have a child and would name him Jesus. Mary was disturbed by this news, and asked how this could be so, since she had no husband. Gabriel told her that the Holy Spirit would come upon her, and she would conceive a son (Lk 1:26–38). This is how Jesus' life on earth began.

In my home, we have a crucifix hanging on the wall in the living room. There's a very large one in my parish church, too. When I see a crucifix, it reminds me that God loves me so much that he sent his Son, Jesus, who died on the cross to heal our sinfulness. Because of the sacrifice Jesus made, I can someday live with God forever in heaven.

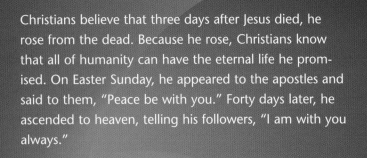

Christians believe that three days after Jesus died, he rose from the dead. Because he rose, Christians know that all of humanity can have the eternal life he promised. On Easter Sunday, he appeared to the apostles and said to them, "Peace be with you." Forty days later, he ascended to heaven, telling his followers, "I am with you always."

Jesus is at the heart of my Christian faith, so I also have a picture of him in my bedroom. The picture helps me remember that Jesus is close to me, even if I can't see him. He's taking care of me, because he loves me. I pray to him, and he teaches me to pray, too.

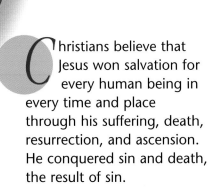

Christians believe that Jesus won salvation for every human being in every time and place through his suffering, death, resurrection, and ascension. He conquered sin and death, the result of sin.

Aisha believes in Jesus too, although she doesn't believe that he is the Son of God. She does believe that he was born of a virgin, Mary, by special divine intervention. Muslims teach that Jesus was a prophet, but that another very important prophet came after him. This prophet's name was Muhammad. Aisha follows the teachings of Muhammad. She prays to God using the words that Muhammad taught Muslims to say.

Muhammad lived in the city of Mecca in what is now Saudi Arabia. At that time, many people visited the city to worship pagan idols, and Muhammad disapproved of this practice. When he was forty years old, while meditating in a desert cave, Muhammad heard a voice that told him to "Proclaim!" Muhammad believed that this voice came from the Angel Gabriel. He shared his experience with others. They came to believe that Allah was calling Muhammad to be a prophet to his people, giving him messages directly through the angel. Muhammad's followers memorized and recorded the messages he was given. These were later collected in the Qur'an.

Muhammad was rejected by many people because he proclaimed a morality and social order that challenged their lifestyles and practices. He taught belief in one God, which threatened the wealth of those who benefited from the commercial aspects of idol worship. Nevertheless, Muhammad continued to proclaim, and Muslims believe he received messages from God for twenty-three years.

The number of people who listened to Muhammad grew, and those who followed him came to be known as Muslims, "those who submit to God."

Muhammad taught that Allah did not want his followers to return to their former ways of idol worship. For this reason, there are no visual depictions of Allah in Islam.

Muslims believe that no artistic representation could adequately reflect the fullness of beauty contained in God and his creation. Islamic art is instead composed of geometric and floral shapes and patterns, and of beautiful Arabic calligraphy, or lettering.

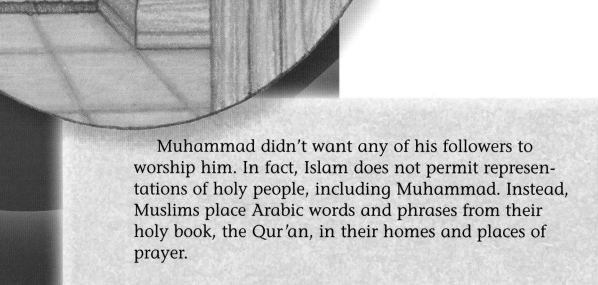

Muhammad didn't want any of his followers to worship him. In fact, Islam does not permit representations of holy people, including Muhammad. Instead, Muslims place Arabic words and phrases from their holy book, the Qur'an, in their homes and places of prayer.

The holy book of the Muslims is called the Qur'an. Sometimes it's spelled "Koran." Muslims believe that the Qur'an is the word of God revealed to the Prophet Muhammad through the Angel Gabriel. Aisha knows parts of several *surahs*, or chapters, of the Qur'an by heart.

God's messages to Muhammad became the Qur'an. The Qur'an was originally recorded in Arabic, and though it has been translated into many other languages, including English, it is always read in Arabic in Muslim prayer. Only about one-sixth of the world's Muslims are Arabic speakers, but because the Qur'an is seen as the word of God, Muslims must read it in its original form.

Observance of Islamic law, or *Shariah,* is also very important. *Shariah* is based on the Qur'an's command to protect the weak, and on *Hadith* (the recorded traditions of Muhammad), as well as *Qiyas* (analogical reasoning) and *Ijma* (consensus). The goal of *Shariah* is to create a just society by regulating the way people act toward each other. It influences the way that Muslims consider family life, crime and punishment, property, business, and morality.

*I*n addition to the Qur'an, indispensable sources for living the Islamic faith include the *Sunnah,* the customary practices of Muhammad recorded in the *Hadith*. Muslims strive to emulate Muhammad.

The sacred book for Christians is the Bible. The Catholic Bible contains the Old Testament (Hebrew Scriptures plus a few other books) and the New Testament (Christian Scriptures). We believe the Bible is God's Word. God inspired human authors to write what he wanted, and God speaks to us today through this book. I memorized some of the Psalms during Vacation Bible School at my parish last summer.

Most of the Old Testament books were written in Hebrew and tell of the covenant that God made with the Jews. The New Testament was originally written in Greek and reveals how God fulfills his covenant with all people through Jesus Christ. The main books of the New Testament are the four Gospels ("gospel" means "good news") and the epistles, or letters, written by the earliest followers of Jesus. Because the stories of Jesus' words and actions were recorded some thirty to sixty years after he died, there are variations in how they are told. Variations also arise because the evangelists were writing for specific communities of faith. The Bible is available in many languages and translations.

Along with Sacred Scripture, to which it is closely related, Sacred Tradition is an essential element of the Catholic faith. Tradition is the living transmission of the message given by Jesus for the Church. The preaching of the apostles and the written messages contained in the Bible are passed on by means of Tradition. Tradition is the way the Church lives the apostolic teaching.

For Catholics, Sacred Tradition and Sacred Scripture together form one sacred deposit of the Word of God.

Muslims have prayer beads that they use to recite the Ninety-Nine Names of Allah, or for invocations such as "May Allah grant pardon."

The Ninety-Nine Names of Allah include "The Compassionate," "The Merciful," "The Most Holy," "The Mighty," "The Protector," and "The Creator."

Although, for Catholics, the only mediator between God and humanity is Jesus Christ, an intercessor is one who prays on behalf of someone else. Catholics, and many other Christians, look to Mary, the Mother of God, and to other saints to intercede for them. Praying the Rosary is a popular Marian devotion that honors Mary and therefore pleases her Son. It involves meditating on twenty sacred mysteries that recall events in the lives of Jesus and Mary while reciting prayers, mostly the Hail Mary. The mysteries are divided into four sets, called the Joyful, Luminous, Sorrowful, and Glorious mysteries. A circle of beads is used to keep count of the prayers that accompany each mystery.

The Qur'an includes many stories that are also found in the Jewish and Christian Scriptures. One story that is found in both the Bible and the Qur'an is the story of the Angel Gabriel's announcement to Mary of the coming birth of Jesus. Both Christians and Muslims believe that Mary was a virgin chosen by God to be the mother of Jesus.

The Bible says: "In the sixth month the angel Gabriel was sent from God to a city of Galilee named Nazareth, to a virgin who was betrothed to a man of the house of David named Joseph, and the virgin's name was Mary. And when he came into her presence he said, 'Hail, full of grace, the Lord is with you!' She was perplexed by these words and wondered what sort of greeting this could be. Then the angel said to her, 'Fear not, Mary—you have found grace before the Lord. And, behold, you will conceive in your womb and will bear a son, and you shall name him Jesus. He will be great and will be called Son of the Most High, and the Lord God will give him the throne of his father, David. He will reign over the house of Jacob forever, and his Kingdom will have no end.' Mary said to the angel, 'How will this come about, since I do not know man?' And in answer the angel said to her, 'The Holy Spirit will come upon you, and the power of the Most High will overshadow you; therefore, the holy child to be born will be called Son of God.' ... Mary said, 'Behold, the handmaid of the Lord; let it be done to me according to your word.' Then the angel left her" (Lk 1:26–35, 38).

The Qur'an says: "Relate in the Book (the story of) Mary, when she withdrew from her family to a place in the East. She placed a screen (to screen herself) from them; then We sent to her Our angel, and he appeared before her as a man in all respects. She said: 'I seek refuge from you to (Allah) Most Gracious: (come not near) if you fear Allah.' He said, 'Nay, I am only a messenger from your Lord, (to announce) to you the gift of a holy son.' She said: 'How shall I have a son, seeing that no man has touched me, and I am not unchaste?' He said: 'So (it will be): your Lord says, 'That is easy for Me: and (We wish) to appoint him as a Sign to men and a Mercy from Us': it is a matter (so) decreed'" (Surah 19: 16–21).

Muslims also revere Mary, but they do not ask for her help and intercession. Muslims pray only to God. There are no intercessors. However, because Muslims believe that Mary is the mother of Jesus, a very important prophet, she has one of the greatest roles in Islam. In addition to being the virgin who bore Jesus, and a woman of immense faith, Muslims believe that Mary is one of four women who are promised paradise. The others are Khadija, the first wife of Muhammad and the first person to accept Islam; Asiya, the wife of Pharoah during the time of Moses and the Exodus; and Fatima, a daughter of Muhammad.

For Christians, sacraments are sacred signs through which Jesus gives grace, God's life. They are religious rites that are rooted in Jesus' earthly ministry. They developed in the early centuries of Christianity and mark important moments in a Christian's life. Catholics celebrate seven sacraments: Baptism, Confirmation, Holy Eucharist, Reconciliation, Anointing of the Sick, Holy Orders, and Matrimony. Some other Christian denominations recognize only Baptism and the Lord's Supper as sacraments.

Christians believe that when Jesus, the Son of God, became man and was born of the Virgin Mary, he made all of creation a new creation. God our Father calls me to turn away from sin and become more like him as I grow. Jesus makes that possible. I'm glad I have my parents to guide me as I grow in my Catholic faith.

*B*aptism, a sacrament of initiation along with Eucharist and Confirmation, is the first and most necessary sacrament. It fills us, who were born with original sin, with grace by uniting us to the death and resurrection of Jesus. Baptism marks each of us permanently as a member of the Church with the right to the other sacraments. Receiving the sacraments helps Catholics grow closer to God.

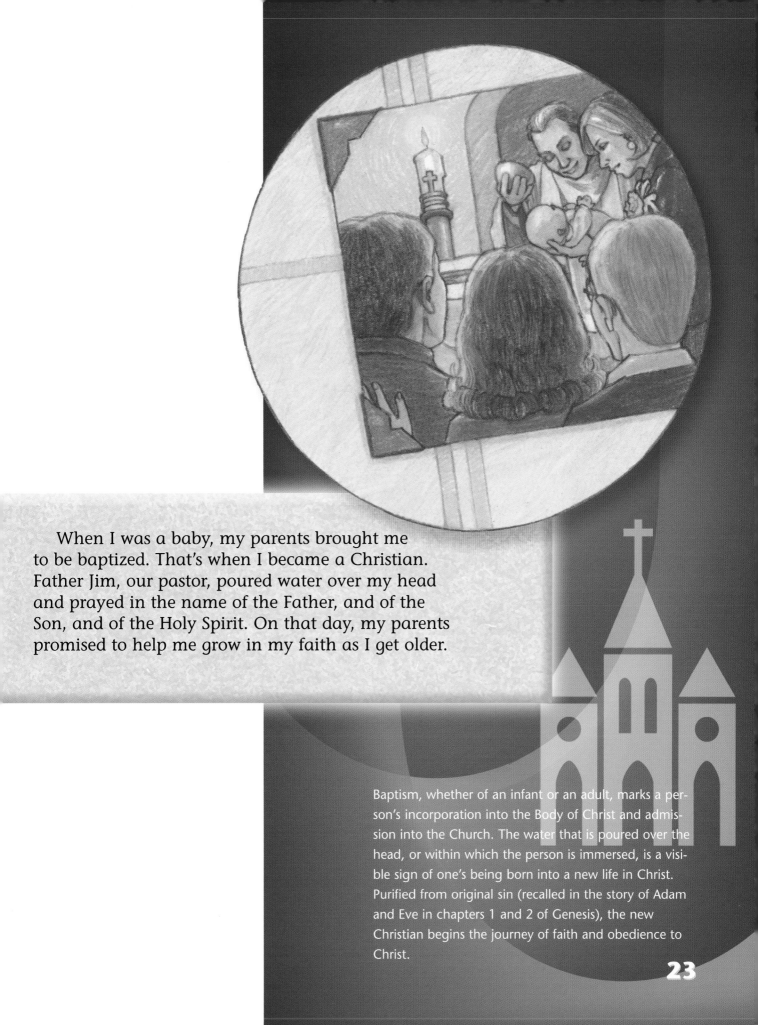

When I was a baby, my parents brought me to be baptized. That's when I became a Christian. Father Jim, our pastor, poured water over my head and prayed in the name of the Father, and of the Son, and of the Holy Spirit. On that day, my parents promised to help me grow in my faith as I get older.

Baptism, whether of an infant or an adult, marks a person's incorporation into the Body of Christ and admission into the Church. The water that is poured over the head, or within which the person is immersed, is a visible sign of one's being born into a new life in Christ. Purified from original sin (recalled in the story of Adam and Eve in chapters 1 and 2 of Genesis), the new Christian begins the journey of faith and obedience to Christ.

Islam has five essential duties, which Muslims call the five pillars of Islam. Like the pillars of a building, they are the supports for the beliefs and practices of the Islamic faith.

The first of the five pillars, and the most important, is the *Shahada*. This statement is the basis for all Muslim belief.

Aisha told me she was born a Muslim. When she was born, her father whispered into her ear the words of the *Adhan,* or call to prayer. This contains the most important element of the Islamic faith, the *Shahada,* and is always recited in Arabic. Muslims believe that the invitation to follow God is one of the first things a newborn should hear.

When children are born into Islam, they grow into their faith as they grow older, learning their religious duties at a very young age. There is no specific ritual of initiation. As a child enters puberty, the religious duties become obligatory, and are believed by Muslims to be recorded by God.

Every Muslim must say, and deeply believe, the words of the *Shahada:* "I bear witness that there is no god but the One God, and I bear witness that Muhammad is His Messenger." In Arabic, it sounds like this: *Ash-hadu an la ilaha illa Allah, wa ash-hadu anna Muhammad ar-rasoolu Allah.* Just as my parents made a promise of faith at my Baptism, Aisha's parents committed themselves when she was born to helping her grow into her Islamic beliefs.

When an adult converts to Islam, that person makes his or her statement of faith, the *Shahada,* with conviction, before witnesses. From this point on, the person is considered a Muslim.

Prayers are offered at five specific times throughout the day: dawn, midday, afternoon, sunset, and at night, before bed. The prayers last only a few minutes and consist of silent or recited prayers and many movements, including bowings and prostrations, to show submission to God. All over the world, Muslims stop whatever they are doing at the designated times of prayer, and face toward Mecca, Islam's holiest city. The prayer is a time of direct contact with God, a time to feel inner peace, happiness, and comfort.

Muslims also communicate with God in their own words, or by reciting prayers that Muhammad prayed and that are not part of the *Salat* obligation. These prayers, called "supplication," can be prayed at any time.

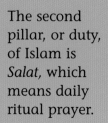

The second pillar, or duty, of Islam is *Salat,* which means daily ritual prayer.

Aisha and I each want to grow in our faiths. We both want to become good and holy, the way God wants us to be. One way we do this is by praying. Every day, Aisha prays five times, as Allah instructed Muhammad to do. To show respect for Allah, she prepares herself to pray by washing her hands, face, arms, and feet. This practice is called "ablutions." When she prays, she faces Mecca, which in the United States is toward the northeast. This is because Allah told Muhammad that Muslims should pray toward the holy city. She kneels down and puts her head to the ground to show that she is honoring and submitting to Allah.

Christian prayer can take place anywhere and at any time. Jesus instructed his followers to pray, taught them the prayer known as the Lord's Prayer, and said that where two or three are gathered in his name, he is present (Mt 18:20).

The official prayer of the Roman Catholic Church is called the Liturgy of the Hours. It is a collection of Scripture passages, hymns, writings of historic Christians, and prayers. The Liturgy of the Hours is composed of five daily prayer times: the Office of Readings, morning prayer, daytime prayer, evening prayer, and night prayer. All priests and many religious are obliged to pray the daily Liturgy of the Hours, and lay members of the Church are encouraged to pray it.

Christians are not obligated to pray at specific times. My family, like many others, always prays before meals, thanking God and asking him to bless us, our time together, and our food. We also pray for those who don't have enough to eat. Sometimes we pray the Rosary together after dinner. Every morning I say a prayer when I wake up, offering the day to God. And at night before I go to sleep I ask God to bless my family and friends and to help me be a better person.

Christian prayer has five forms: adoration, praise, thanksgiving, repentance, and petition.

When Jesus was preparing for his approaching death, he shared his last meal with his closest followers. Christians call this the "Last Supper." During the meal, Jesus changed bread and wine into his Body and Blood, although they still had the appearance of bread and wine. Then he gave them to his disciples. He asked them to continue to celebrate this special meal in remembrance of him after his death. At every Mass, Jesus' sacrifice for our sins, offered at the Last Supper and at Calvary, is made present so that we can offer him and ourselves to the Father.

Catholics believe that when the priest prays over the bread and wine during the Mass, they become, through the power of the Holy Spirit, the actual Body and Blood of Jesus Christ. Jesus is present as both God and man. This change is called "transubstantiation."

Every week, my family and I go to our parish church for Sunday Mass. We hear the Word of God in the Scripture readings that the lector and the priest proclaim. We also receive the Eucharist, the Body and Blood of Jesus under the forms of bread and wine. We sing and pray with our community of faith.

It's important for everyone to participate in the liturgy of the Mass. Sometimes my brother and I help as altar servers, and at Christmas and Easter I like to sing in the junior choir. My father is an usher, so he welcomes people as they arrive at church and helps them find a place to sit.

Did you know?

Eucharist means "thanksgiving."

Like their Jewish ancestors in the faith, Christians observe the Sabbath. For Jews the Lord's Day is Saturday. Because Jesus rose from the dead on the "eighth day," and because Pentecost, the day the Holy Spirit came down upon the Church, occurred on Sunday, Christians made this day the Lord's Day.

Catholics are obliged to participate at Mass, the Eucharistic Celebration, on Sunday or on Saturday evening, the vigil. They gather to worship together, to thank God, and to remember and enter into the death and resurrection of Jesus, which saved us. Through Communion, Catholics are united with Jesus and with one another. For all these reasons, the Eucharist is the source and summit of Catholic life.

As the place where the Islamic community gathers to pray, the mosque has special rooms for performing ablutions. There are rooms for studying and for teaching the children. Mosques are open throughout the day, and many Muslims come to pray individually as well as at the designated times for community prayer. Muslims are happy to give tours of their places of worship, which are also centers for family, for social life, and for education.

The place where Muslims worship as a community of believers is called a mosque, pronounced *mosk*. Aisha's family goes to the mosque for midday prayers every Friday. They hear selections read from the Qur'an, and a sermon is given by the Imam, or prayer leader. Then they all pray.

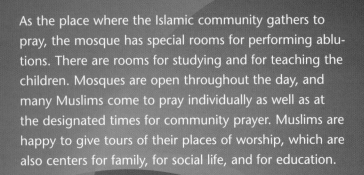

The Arabic word for mosque, *masjid,* means simply "place of prostration." Therefore, strictly speaking, a *masjid* need not be a building.

30

Some Muslim women choose not to wear the *hijab,* or headscarf, all the time. However, to show reverence for God, they are required to wear it for prayer.

Muslim men are required to gather at the mosque for Friday prayer. Many Muslim women also choose to pray at the mosque. Aisha's father and brother pray on the main floor, and Aisha and her mother pray upstairs in the balcony, since men and women usually pray in different areas of the mosque to maintain modesty. Aisha also attends Islamic classes, which her mother teaches once a week.

Did you know?

In Muslim-majority countries, Friday is usually a holiday from work.

Muslims remove their shoes before entering the prayer areas, in order to keep the carpet of the sacred space of prayer clean. It is important that Muslim prayer be made in a clean space.

Friday is the holy day of Muslims. After Friday prayers, Muslims typically visit one another and socialize.

Easter is the most important of the Christian celebrations. Catholics celebrate the great mysteries of redemption with the Paschal Triduum, three days of special prayer. The Triduum begins the evening of Holy Thursday with the celebration of the Lord's Last Supper, and continues on Good Friday, reaching its highest point in the Easter Vigil Saturday evening, and concluding with evening prayer on Easter Sunday. During this time, as well as during the season of Lent, Catholics focus on the events leading up to the death and resurrection of Jesus.

Christians celebrate the birth of Jesus on Christmas, December 25. Christmas brings wonderful traditions, such as Midnight Mass on Christmas Eve, gift-giving, and caroling.

But the greatest feast of our year is Easter Sunday. Jesus never sinned, but he was tortured and forced to die on a cross like a criminal. Jesus gave us a great gift in accepting this death out of love for all mankind. But even this was not all that God gave us in Jesus, his Son. Jesus rose from the dead. On Easter, the tomb is empty, and Jesus offers us a new life with him forever!

Did you know?

Easter is celebrated each year in March or April on the first Sunday after the first full moon of spring.

We prepare for Easter with the season of Lent. On Ash Wednesday, we receive blessed ashes on our foreheads. These ashes remind us that someday we will die. They remind us to live a good life and to do penance. During Lent, we prepare to celebrate Jesus' resurrection by trying to receive the sacrament of Reconciliation more often. We also make small sacrifices—I give up candy and try to be nicer to my brother!

When we're fourteen or older, we don't eat meat on Ash Wednesday and on all Fridays in Lent, to honor Jesus' sacrifice for us. When we're eighteen or older, we also fast on Ash Wednesday and Good Friday, eating only one full meal. The other two meals together should not equal a full one, and we avoid snacking. On Easter, we have a big feast to celebrate Jesus' resurrection!

*T*he season of Lent prepares candidates for Baptism and assists all Catholics in renewing their baptismal commitment.

Lent is a period of forty days, not counting Sundays. It is a time of spiritual preparation for the Easter Triduum, a time when Christians give more attention to prayer, penance, and good deeds. Purple is the color of the priests' vestments during Lent. The music at Mass is more somber than usual, and the Gloria and Alleluia, both expressions of joy, are omitted from the liturgical celebration.

The Islamic calendar has twelve months, 354 days. The ninth month is one of the most significant of the year. Because Muslims believe that it was during this month that Muhammad received the first revelations that eventually formed the Qur'an, they spend extra time studying and reciting from the Qur'an during Ramadan. All Muslims who are fit, healthy, and have reached the age of puberty are obligated to fast during Ramadan.

Muslims live their religion based on a lunar calendar, which means that they determine their celebrations by cycles of the moon. During the ninth month of the Islamic calendar, Muslims observe a very special month called Ramadan. During every day of this month, they fast from food and drink during daylight hours. Meals are eaten only before dawn and after sunset. Aisha told me she and her family take more time to pray during the month of Ramadan. They concentrate more on their love and need for God, and also become more aware of the needs of others.

Since the lunar year is shorter than the solar year, Ramadan begins about eleven days earlier each solar year than the year before. It can therefore occur in different seasons. Because fasting takes place during daylight hours, the fast is more difficult during summer than in wintertime.

During Ramadan, Muslims commemorate the night when they believe that the Qur'an was revealed and the Prophet Muhammad first heard the voice of the Angel Gabriel. This night is called *Lailat al-Qadr,* or the Night of Power, and falls toward the end of the month. Muslims try to stay awake during this night, often in the mosque, praying and reading from the Qur'an.

The month of Ramadan concludes with a three-day celebration, and of course a feast! As soon as the new moon is sighted, the fasting of Ramadan stops and Muslims prepare for *Eid al-Fitr,* a celebration that occurs after the end of Ramadan. Wealthy families give food and donations to poorer families at this time so that everyone has a joyful celebration. Aisha's family invites the elderly couple that lives near them to join their family for the day.

Fasting during the month of Ramadan is *Sawm,* the third of the five pillars of Islam.

Muslims show kindness to those who are less fortunate by offering them charity. Muslims who are able to do so give 2 1/2 percent of their net income and of all they own to help people who are poor. In many Islamic countries, the mosques are responsible for distributing the money to those in need.

Aisha's family helps their neighbors often. The elderly couple next door has no living children. Once when I was at Aisha's house, her mother asked us to go over to visit Mr. and Mrs. Kuofi and bring a casserole she had baked, along with some fresh dates. She gave us an envelope of money for them, too, because they aren't well off financially. Aisha's parents also make donations at the mosque to help people who are less fortunate.

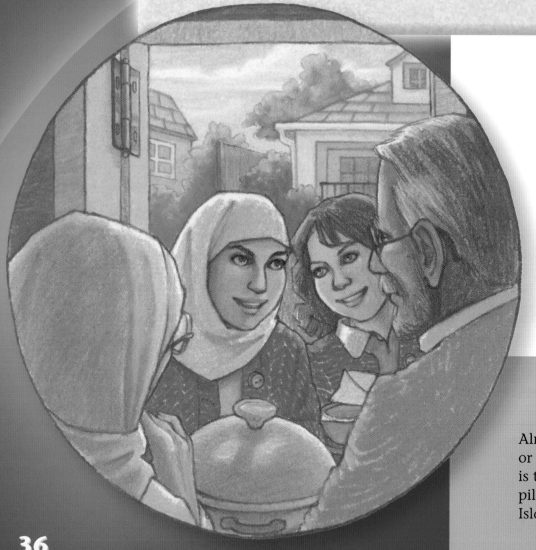

Almsgiving, or *Zakat*, is the fourth pillar of Islam.

Did you know?

Both Muslims and Christians hope to bring the goodness of God to others through their own lives.

The Catholic Church defines acts of charity that are done for the benefit of others as "works of mercy." The corporal works of mercy are based on the Gospel of Matthew (25:31–46), and include feeding the hungry, sheltering the homeless, clothing the naked, visiting the sick and imprisoned, and burying the dead. The spiritual works of mercy include comforting the sorrowful, bearing wrongs patiently, forgiving injuries, and praying for the living and the dead.

Christians are also called to "be Christ to one another," in challenging practices of society that marginalize the poor and prevent them from overcoming their poverty, and in living lives that bring hope, peace, justice, and love to others.

My family gives alms, too. Every week, my mother writes a check that she puts into the collection basket at church. I save part of my allowance and put that into the basket, too. These donations help with the upkeep of our parish. Our parish family also supports many good works, such as a food pantry that provides groceries for those who need assistance, as well as a drop-in center for teens.

My own family does something special each Lent to help less fortunate people. This year, we served lunch each Saturday to residents of our city's homeless shelter.

The fifth and last pillar of Islam is the *Hajj*, or pilgrimage.

If it is financially and physically possible, every Muslim makes a pilgrimage to Mecca at least once. A pilgrimage is a special journey to a place that is sacred. Aisha hasn't gone to Mecca yet, but her parents have, and so has her older brother. Every year, at a specific time, the pilgrims travel to Mecca from all around the world. They worship together like members of one family. The pilgrimage is a very special event for Muslims.

The *Hajj* takes place only during the second week of the twelfth lunar month. During the *Hajj* Muslims visit the *Kaaba*, a cube-shaped stone shrine covered in black velvet and gold needlework. The *Kaaba* was built by Muhammad and his son Ishmael for the worship of the one God.

The *Kaaba* has been rebuilt several times, and still contains a sacred black stone. Muslim pilgrims to Mecca circle around the *Kaaba* counterclockwise seven times, which symbolizes the centrality of God in Islam. They also travel between two small mountains seven times. This journey, which represents the struggles of life, imitates that of Hagar, the mother of Ishmael, as she desperately searched for water in the desert. The well of Zamzam, from which pilgrims usually take a ritual drink, is said to have sprung up as the infant Ishmael struck the earth with his feet. Many pilgrims bring some of the water from the well home with them after their *Hajj*.

*Eid al-Adha, t*he Feast of the Sacrifice, takes place during the *Hajj*. It commemorates the sacrifice of Abraham.

Christians aren't required to make pilgrimages, but many do visit shrines and sacred places in the Holy Land, Rome, and around the world. Before he and my mother met, my father went to France to visit the Lourdes Shrine, where the Blessed Mother appeared to Saint Bernadette. Dad said that his pilgrimage helped him to more fully understand the power of the sacrament of Baptism, and made him want to be a better Christian. He also believes that Mary led him to my mother, because he prayed at the shrine that God would help him find a good wife, and he met Mom shortly after that!

Did you know?

Catholic shrines are located all over the world. They each encourage devotion to a particular saint or Christian mystery.

Many Christian pilgrims request a special grace, a gift undeserved by humans but given freely by God to aid toward growing in holiness. Some may pray for a particular intention. Some make pilgrimages to ask for God's forgiveness, and others to offer thanks to God.

The Lourdes Shrine in France was built after a series of eighteen apparitions occurred between February 11 and July 16, 1858, to a young girl named Bernadette Soubirous. During one apparition, the Virgin Mary announced, "I am the Immaculate Conception." This confirmed the doctrine, declared four years earlier, that Mary was conceived without original sin. Mary directed Bernadette to a spring of water around which the shrine was later built. Many associate the waters with miraculous healings attributed to the intercession of Mary. Pilgrims often take some of the water from the spring home with them.

Islam does not permit terrorism. The Qur'an is the basis for the Muslim belief that inciting terror in the hearts of defenseless civilians, and destroying property and innocent people, are forbidden and detestable acts. Muslims who would use terror to control others in the name of Allah are radical extremists who rationalize their actions by distorting the teachings of Islam.

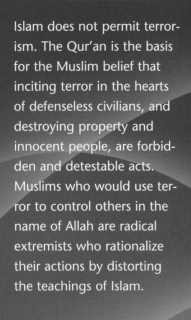

Many Americans learn about Islam only from the news reports they see on television. Terrorism has hurt a lot of people, and because some terrorists claim to be acting in the name of Islam, there are those who mistakenly believe that all Muslims are associated with terrorism.

A stereotype is an oversimplified label that people give to a group. Stereotypes are often untrue or only partly true. I've learned that not all Muslims are the same, and you can't apply stereotypes to them. There are lots of Muslims who live their lives in prayer and in peace, the way Aisha and her family do.

The vast majority of Muslims have nothing to do with violent acts of terrorism. Many Muslims leaders speak out against terrorism, expressing hope for peace.

Aisha's religion desires more than anything else to bring all people to the peaceful worship of the one God. "Islam" means surrender to God. Surrendering everything to God and faithfully living the Islamic devotion to prayer helps Muslims to be peaceful people themselves and to promote peace among others.

The message Jesus Christ gave when he lived on earth was a message of love. Jesus continues to call Christians to "love one another as I have loved you," and he gives us the strength and the ability to reach out to offer others an expression of God's love.

The Catholic Church, in a document titled *Nostra Aetate (Declaration on the Relation of the Church to Non-Christian Religions)* from the Second Vatican Council in 1965, states:

"In our time, when ... mankind is being drawn closer together, and the ties between different peoples are becoming stronger, the Church examines more closely her relationship to non-Christian religions. In her task of promoting unity and love among men, ... she considers ... what men have in common and what draws them to fellowship.... Since in the course of centuries not a few quarrels and hostilities have arisen between Christians and [Muslims], this sacred synod urges all to forget the past and to work sincerely for mutual understanding and to preserve as well as to promote together for the benefit of all mankind social justice and moral welfare, as well as peace and freedom."

There are plenty of differences between Islam and Christianity, just as there are between Aisha and me. But Aisha and I have a lot in common, too, and so do our religions. I'm glad I know Aisha. I've learned from her what Islam is all about, and she's learned about my Catholic faith from me. We're lucky to have each other, and we're happy to be friends!

For Catholic Parents:

If your son or daughter has a Muslim student in his or her class, welcome the opportunity to learn about another world religion. Encourage your child to befriend the student.

If your child has a Muslim friend, treat that friend as you would any other child. When a Muslim visits your home, remember that he or she may not be familiar with Catholic practices. When your family engages in religious customs such as meal prayers, be sure to briefly explain what you're doing. Don't avoid any usual religious practices when a Muslim is visiting, but take advantage of the opportunity to share information about your faith, and also to learn about Islam.

Be sensitive to the customs of the Muslim child. If the child is staying overnight, ask if you can provide a private place for prayer before bedtime and upon awakening.

When a Muslim joins you for a meal, don't serve any type of pork or pork products. Muslims do not eat pork or drink alcohol.

For Catholic Teachers:

If you have Muslim students in your school, be sure to provide a space for them to pray. It should be as private as possible, quiet, and clean. Your student may need to wash before praying. Try to schedule classes to allow time for Muslim students to pray without disrupting the established classroom routine; prayers generally can be completed in ten to fifteen minutes.

Be sure to explain Christian customs, traditions, and celebrations clearly. Provide your Christian students with an example of how to respect diversity.

Seek out ways to observe Ramadan with Muslim students. Some schools offer a day of fasting as an experience for all students to share. Younger Muslim children are not obliged to fast, but many do. Naturally, it's important to approach fasting with common sense, especially when students are engaged in physical activities and sports. Nevertheless, there may be some small way to encourage students to give up candy, soda, or eating between meals to mark Ramadan for at least one day. The money saved can be collected and the Muslim students consulted to determine the recipient of the donation. In this way, Muslims will not be isolated in their religious practices, and Christian students will have an opportunity to share in the Islamic experience. Similar learning opportunities could be offered to Muslim students during Lent.

Mark celebrations of Islam and other world religions on the classroom calendar. Ask Muslim students or their parents to make a short presentation to educate the class about their religious practices. Arrange a field trip to tour the local mosque.

For Parents and Teachers:

Read the Second Vatican Council document *Nostra Aetate (Declaration on the Relation of the Church to Non-Christian Religions),* and act on the attitudes of openness and respect it promotes.

Resources for Children

Barnes, Trevor. *The Kingfisher Book of Religions: Festivals, Ceremonies, and Beliefs from Around the World.* New York, NY: Kingfisher, 1999.

Meredith, Susan. *The Usborne Book of World Religions.* Tulsa, OK: EDC, 1995.

Osborne, Mary Pope. *One World, Many Religions: The Ways We Worship.* New York, NY: Knopf, 1996.

Resources for Adults

Armour, Rollin, Sr. *Islam, Christianity, and the West: A Troubled History.* Maryknoll, NY: Orbis Books, 2002.

Catoir, John T. *World Religions: Beliefs Behind Today's Headlines.* Rev. ed. Staten Island, NY: Alba House, 2004.

Eerdman's Handbook to the World's Religions. Rev. ed. Grand Rapids, MI: Wm. B. Eerdman's, 1994.

Esposito, John. *Islam, the Straight Path.* 3rd ed. New York: Oxford University Press, 1998.

Funk, Mary Margaret. *Islam Is...An Experience of Dialogue and Devotion.* New York: Lantern Books, 2003.

Jomier, Jacques. *The Bible and the Qur'an.* San Francisco, CA: Ignatius, 2002.

————. *How to Understand Islam.* New York, NY: Crossroad, 1989.

Milot, Jean-René. *Muslims and Christians: Enemies or Brothers?* Staten Island, NY: Alba House, 1997.

Paul VI. *Nostra Aetate (Declaration on the Relation of the Church to Non-Christian Religions).* October 28, 1965. Vatican website: http://www.vatican.va/archive/hist_councils/ii_vatican_council/documents/vat-ii_decl_19651028_nostra-aetate_en.html (accessed February 1, 2006).

Renard, John. *Responses to 101 Questions on Islam.* Mahwah, NJ: Paulist, 1998.

Waines, David. *An Introduction to Islam.* 2nd ed. Cambridge: Cambridge University Press, 2003.

Wilkins, Ronald J. *Religions of the World.* Dubuque, IA: Brown-Roa, 1995.

Acknowledgments

This book began as a class project to apply the values and content of interreligious dialogue to everyday life. With the hope that this book will influence, even in a very small way, relationships that foster understanding between Christians and Muslims in our world today, I would like to thank those who worked with me to transform my initial effort into the book you are holding now: Fr. Richard L. Schebera, SMM, Ph.D., for his course on interreligious dialogue at St. Louis University and for his personal integrity; Mary Martha Moss, FSP, for her encouragement and her example of what we can accomplish; Mary Joseph Peterson, FSP, for her inspired book design; and Diane Lynch, my editor at Pauline Books & Media, for her enthusiasm and dedication to this project.

To all those who were kind enough to make suggestions regarding the text, especially Archbishop Michael Fitzgerald, M.Afr.; Rev. Canon Francis Tiso, Ph.D.; Dr. Asma Mobin-Uddin; John Renard, Ph.D.; Sandra Keating, Ph.D.; Joe Pribyl; Kathleen Glavich, SND; Edilma Hosein; Susan Abbott; Fr. David Michael; and Marianne Lorraine Trouvé, FSP, I offer my heartfelt thanks.

Donna Jean Kemmetmueller, FSP

Pauline
BOOKS & MEDIA

The Daughters of St. Paul operate book and media centers at the following addresses. Visit, call or write the one nearest you today, or find us on the World Wide Web, www.pauline.org

California
3908 Sepulveda Blvd, Culver City, CA 90230	310-397-8676
2640 Broadway Street, Redwood City, CA 94063	650-369-4230
5945 Balboa Avenue, San Diego, CA 92111	858-565-9181

Florida
145 S.W. 107th Avenue, Miami, FL 33174	305-559-6715

Hawaii
1143 Bishop Street, Honolulu, HI 96813	808-521-2731
Neighbor Islands call:	866-521-2731

Illinois
172 North Michigan Avenue, Chicago, IL 60601	312-346-4228

Louisiana
4403 Veterans Memorial Blvd, Metairie, LA 70006	504-887-7631

Massachusetts
885 Providence Hwy, Dedham, MA 02026	781-326-5385

Missouri
9804 Watson Road, St. Louis, MO 63126	314-965-3512

New Jersey
561 U.S. Route 1, Wick Plaza, Edison, NJ 08817	732-572-1200

New York
150 East 52nd Street, New York, NY 10022	212-754-1110

Pennsylvania
9171-A Roosevelt Blvd, Philadelphia, PA 19114	215-676-9494

South Carolina
243 King Street, Charleston, SC 29401	843-577-0175

Tennessee
4811 Poplar Avenue, Memphis, TN 38117	901-761-2987

Texas
114 Main Plaza, San Antonio, TX 78205	210-224-8101

Virginia
1025 King Street, Alexandria, VA 22314	703-549-3806

Canada
3022 Dufferin Street, Toronto, ON M6B 3T5	416-781-9131